PIERCE-ARROW

BOOKS BY SUSAN HOWE

POETRY

Hinge Picture, Telephone Books, 1974

The Western Borders, Tuumba Press, 1976

Secret History of the Dividing Line, Telephone Books, 1979

Cabbage Gardens, Fathom Press, 1979

The Liberties, 1980

Pythagorean Silence, The Montemora Foundation, 1982

Defenestration of Prague, The Kulcher Foundation, 1983

Articulation of Sound Forms in Time, Awede Press, 1987

A Bibliography of the King's Book or, Eikon Basilike, Paradigm Press, 1989

The Europe of Trusts: Selected Poems, Sun & Moon Press, 1990

Singularities, Wesleyan University Press, 1990

The Nonconformist's Memorial, New Directions, 1993

Frame Structures: Early Poems 1974–1979, New Directions, 1996

CRITICISM

My Emily Dickinson, North Atlantic Books, 1985

Incloser, Weaslesleeves Press, 1985

The Birth-mark: unsettling the wilderness in American literary history,
Wesleyan University Press, 1993

PIERCE-ARROW

SUSAN HOWE

A NEW DIRECTIONS BOOK

A poetry fellowship from the John Simon Guggenheim Memorial Foundation in 1996 gave me time to begin the poems in this selection, and a fellowship from the Stanford Institute of the Humanities during winter 1998 allowed me the time to finish it.

I would like to express my appreciation to Tom Ford for his help at the Houghton Library, Harvard University, and to Graham Foust and Alan Gilbert for their help in the final production. —S.H.

"Rückenfigur" first appeared in *Conjunctions* and portions of "Arisbe" in *The Chicago Review*, *Profession 1998*, *Close Listening: Poetry and the Performed Word*, ed. Charles Bernstein (Oxford University Press, 1998).

Book design by Sylvia Frezzolini Severance
Manufactured in the United States of America
New Directions Books are printed on acid-free paper.
First published as New Directions Paperbook 878 in 1999
Published simultaneously in Canada by Penguin Books Canada Limited

Library of Congress Cataloging-in-Publication Data

Howe, Susan
        Pierce-arrow: poems / by Susan Howe
            p.   cm.
        ISBN 0-8112-1410-9 (pbk.)
        I. Title
    PS3558.0893P5   1999
    811'.54—dc21   98-47300
                                              CIP

New Directions Books are published for James Laughlin
by New Directions Publishing Corporation,
80 Eighth Avenue, New York 10011

For David

Constellations fall across

late field hour toward the green

wood unknown quiet of you

Distance is here to go home

to visit the country early

Morning coming everything home

because love is in the mind

CONTENTS

LIST OF ILLUSTRATIONS

Most of the illustrations reproduced in this book are from the original manuscripts of Charles Sanders Peirce now at the Houghton Library. They are not shot from microfilm copies or photocopies. Some are from notebooks containing existential graphs, others are from separate pages organized and grouped together by later scholars, philosophers, and editors; chronology is mixed. Putting thought in motion to define art in a way that includes science, these graphs, charts, prayers, and tables are free to be drawings, even poems.

In 1905, reviewing *What Is Meaning?* by the English philosopher Victoria Lady Welby for *The Nation*, Peirce wrote: "She urges that people do not sufficiently take to heart the ethics of language. She thinks that modern conceptions call for a modern imagery of speech. But we fear that she does not realize how deep the knife would have to go into the body of speech to make it really scientific. We should have to use words like those the chemists use—if they can be called words."

Perhaps the Word, giving rise to all pictures and graphs, is at the center of Peirce's philosophy. There always was and always will be a secret affinity between symbolic logic and poetry.

ACKNOWLEDGMENTS

This entire book contains material from the manuscripts of Charles Sanders Peirce at Harvard University's Houghton Library: *Charles S. Peirce Papers 1859–1913* (inclusive), [Microform] Film misc. 948 (Harvard University Microreproduction Service, Fall 1964). Excerpts are referred to by catalogue numbers assigned in Richard S. Robin's *An Annotated Catalogue of the Papers of Charles S. Peirce* (Amherst: University of Massachusetts Press, 1967).

Illustrations by Charles S. Peirce are reproduced by permission of the Houghton Library, Harvard University: MS 277 on page 4; MS 278 on pages 114–15; MS 494 on pages xii–xiii and 2; MS 1538 on pages 31, 70, and 117; and MS 1643 on page 1. The manuscript drafts by A. C. Swinburne on pages 43, 45, 46, and 122, from Gen MSS 303, are reproduced by permission of the Beinecke Rare Book and Manuscript Library, Yale University. The autograph signature by A. C. Swinburne on page 32 is from John S. Mayfield, *Swinburneana: A Gallimaufry of Bits and Pieces about Algernon Charles Swinburne* (Gaithersburg, MD: The Waring Press, 1974). The silhouette of George Meredith on page 37 is from Lady Butcher, *Memories of George Meredith, O. M.* (London: Constable and Co., Ltd. 1919).

"Arisbe" is indebted to Joseph Brent's *Charles Sanders Peirce: A Life* (Bloomington: Indiana University Press, 1993); Kenneth Laine Ketner's *His Glassy Essence: An Autobiography of Charles Sanders Peirce* (Nashville: Vanderbilt University Press, 1998); and Elizabeth Walther's *Charles Sanders Peirce: Leben und Werk* (Baden-Baden: Agis-Verlag, 1989). The letter on page 7 is taken directly from *John Jay Chapman and His Letters*, ed. M. A. DeWolfe Howe (Boston: Houghton Mifflin, 1937). A portion of a letter from Henry James, Jr., to Henry S. Leonard is numbered L 723 in Robin's *Annotated Catalogue*. A portion of Ketner's index has been copied directly on page 11. Alexander Pope's translation of the *Iliad of Homer*, Book VI, lines 15-24, is quoted on page 15. The Joseph Addison quote on page 16 and the lines from Pope on page 17 are taken from John Dixon Hunt's *The Figure in the Landscape: Poetry, Painting, and Gardening during the Eighteenth Century* (Baltimore: Johns Hopkins University Press, 1976). Portions of a biographical form written by Peirce for *Men of Science in the United States* (MS 1611) appear on pages 7, 17, and 19.

In "The Leisure of the Theory Class," the exchange between Bruno Lind and George Santayana is taken almost directly from Bruno Lind's *Vagabond Scholar: A Venture into the Privacy of George Santayana* (New York: Bridgehead Books, 1962). Uncited excerpts from Peirce's diary appear on page 14.

praises to

Fig. 99

praises to

Fig. 100

praises to

Fig. 101

praises to

Fig. 102

praises to

Fig. 103

praises to

Fig. 104

praises to

Fig. 105

praises to

Fig. 106

praises to

Fig. 107

praises to

Fig. 108

praises to

Fig. 109

praises to

Fig. 111.

praises to

Fig. 112

praises to

Fig. 110

praises to

Fig. 114

praises to

Fig. 115

praises to

Fig. 113

praises to

Fig. 117

praises to

Fig. 118

praises to

Fig. 116

praises to

Fig. 119

praises to

Fig. 120.

praises to

Fig. 121

praises to

Fig. 122

Fig. 99 Somebody praises somebody to his face
" 100 Somebody does not praise everybody to his face
" 101 Somebody is not praised to his face by anybody
" 102 Somebody does not praise anybody to his face
" 103 Nobody praises anybody to his face
" 104 Somebody is praised to his face by all men
" 105 Somebody praises all men to their faces
" 106 Everybody praises everybody to his face
" 107 Everybody is praised to his face by somebody or other
" 108 Everybody praises somebody or other to his face
" 109 Nobody is praised to his face by all men
" 110. Nobody praises all men to their faces
" 111. Somebody praises somebody within himself
" 112 Somebody does not within himself praise everybody
" 113 Somebody within himself praises no man
" 114 There is somebody whom no all men within himself praises.
" 115 Nobody within himself praises anybody
" 116 Somebody within himself praises all men
" 117 There is a man whom all men within themselves praise
" 118 Everybody within himself praises everybody
" 119 Everybody within himself praises somebody
" 120 Everybody is praised by somebody or other to that persons self
" 121 Nobody within himself praises all men
" 122 There is nobody whom all men praise within themselves.

ARISBE

He loved logic

—Juliette Peirce.

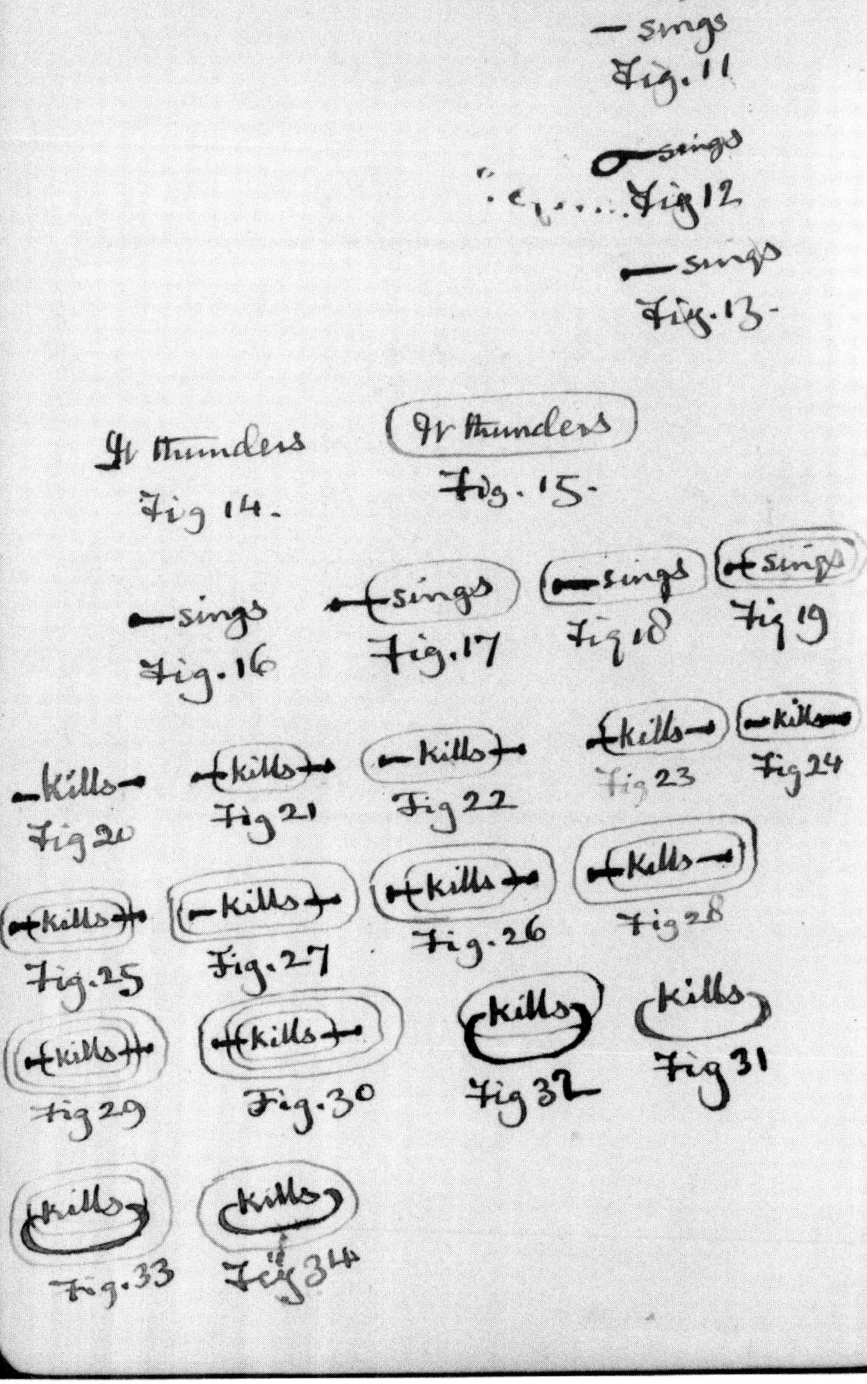

— sings
Fig. 11

— sings
Fig 12

— sings
Fig. 13 -

It thunders
Fig 14.

It thunders
Fig. 15.

— sings
Fig. 16

— sings
Fig. 17

— sings
Fig 18

— sings
Fig 19

— kills —
Fig 20

— kills —
Fig 21

— kills —
Fig 22

— kills —
Fig 23

— kills
Fig 24

— kills —
Fig. 25

— kills —
Fig. 27

— kills —
Fig. 26

— kills —
Fig 28

— kills —
Fig 29

— kills —
Fig. 30

kills
Fig 32

kills
Fig 31

kills
Fig. 33

kills
Fig 34

Phenomenology of war in the *Iliad*

how men appear to each other when

gods change the appearance of things

Send him down unwilling Captain of

the Scorned he is singularly doomed

Mortality is a sign for humanity our

barbarous ancestors my passion-self

Each assertion must maintain its icon

Faith in proof drives him downward

The First Chapter of Logic.

O Creator out of blank nothing of this
Universe whose ▪ immense reality, sublimity,
and beauty so little thrills me as it should,
inspire me with the earnest desire to make
this chapter useful to my brethren!

The earliest occupation of man is poetizing,
~~The info~~ is Feeling and delighting in feeling. That
is what the infant in his cradle seems ~~to be doing~~
mainly ~~to be~~ about.

But feeling ~~pa gives birth~~ generates to dreams; dreams,
desires; desires, impulses to do things. So the
main business of a normal man's ~~life comes~~ comes to
~~be action consists in~~ Action.

But ~~action soon makes~~ any man that
has any ~~ripening power potentiality of~~
~~possibility~~ ability to ripen is soon made by
~~a life of action~~ active life to realize that
his different acts must not stand each for
itself, unrelated to the others, that mere action
is ~~fatuous~~ unless it accomplishes some thing

4

During the summer of 1997 I spent many hours in New Haven in the bow-els of Sterling Library because that's where the microform room is, almost underground, next to preservation. In an adjoining, more cryptlike corridor, behind some discarded, hopelessly outdated computer terminals and micro-film viewers (nothing from the outside or inside will ever be seen on them again) the 38-reel *Charles S. Peirce Papers 1859-1913 (inclusive), [Micro-form] Film misc. 948* is packed inside two drawers of a slate-gray metal file cabinet. No one stays for long in this passage or chamber because it's freez-ing and the noise from air-conditioning generators the university recently installed in a sub-basement immediately underneath resembles roaring or loud sobbing.

Suppose a man is locked in a

room and does not want to go

out his staying is voluntary

is he at liberty no necessity

What shall we finally say if

Members of the Department of

Philosophy Harvard University

undertake the task of sorting

his papers now in the custody

of Harvard's Houghton Library

The microform room at Sterling has several new microfilm readers with Xerox copiers attached. At the left of each viewing screen there is a thin slot for a copy card. Above each slot five singular electric letters spell H E L L O in red as if to confide affection

in all their minute and terrible detail these five little icons could be teeth.

A microphotograph is a type of photograph nearly as old as photography itself, in which an original document is reproduced in a size too small to be read by the naked eye so here the human mind can understand far from it. Film in the form of a strip 16 or 35 millimeters wide bearing a photographic record on a reduced scale of printed or other graphic matter for storage or transmission in a small space is enlarged to be read on a reading machine combining a light source and screen together in a compact cabinet. The original remains perfect by being perfectly what it is because you can't touch it.

Upstairs at the circulation desk, an employee has put a nondescript signal on the horizontal black strip that bisects the verso oblong surface of my white plastic YALE UNIVERSITY LIBRARIES (Lux et Veritas) copy card so the space the cut encloses now represents five dollars. As if invisibility is the only reality on the rapid highway of mechanical invention H E L L O draws card number 156186 inside itself with a hiss.

It is strange how the dead appear in dreams where another space provides our living space as well. Another language another way of speaking so quietly always there in the shape of memories, thoughts, feelings, which are extra-marginal outside of primary consciousness, yet must be classed as some sort of unawakened finite infinite articulation. Documents resemble people talking in sleep. To exist is one thing, to be perceived another. I can spread historical information, words and words we can never touch hovering around subconscious life where enunciation is born, in distinction from what it enunciates when nothing rests in air when what is knowledge?

A person throws a stone

as fact through air not

fact but appearance of

fact floating in vacuua

Blind existential being

may possibly not occur

at all we know nothing

with absolute certainty

of existent things not even

the single "word" <u>the</u>

NAME IN FULL: Charles S. Peirce (I am variously listed in print as Charles Santiago Peirce, Charles Saunders Peirce, and Charles Sanders Peirce. Under the circumstances a noncommital S. suits me best) [MS 1611]. PIERCE *v*; to run into or through as an instrument or pointed weapon does. PURSE *n*; a small bag closed with a drawstring and used to carry money. Even if he trained himself to be ambidextrous and could amaze his undergraduate classmates at Harvard by writing a question on the blackboard with one hand while simultaneously answering it with the other, P<u>ee</u>r/se pronounced <u>Purr</u>/se blamed most of his problems on his own left-handedness.

1893: JOHN JAY CHAPMAN to MRS. HENRY WHITMAN: Charles Peirce wrote the definition of University in the Century Dictionary. He called it an institution for purposes of study. They wrote to him that their notion had been that a university was an institution for instruction. He wrote back that if they had any such notion they were grievously mistaken, that a university had not and never had had anything to do with instruction and that until we got over this idea we should not have any university in this country. He commended Johns Hopkins.

Difficulty increases success

in the moral world why do

we exist at all the end of life

all commerce with the world

What is logic? To understand

you must first read the book

—Sir Proteus

The abrupt dismissal of Charles Sanders Peirce by the trustees of the Johns Hopkins University from his position there as part-time lecturer in logic and literature (1879-84), for reasons never fully explained, might be termed a form of banishment. In spite of clear knowledge that he was a profoundly original thinker, an effective, often charismatic teacher, in spite of the efforts of William James, who consistently recommended him for academic positions at Harvard University, the University of Chicago, and elsewhere, after 1884 Peirce was never again offered another teaching appointment. Scattered rumors and slanders (many of them continue to this day) variously represent America's great logician, the founder of pragmatism and one of the founders of mathematic, or symbolic, logic, as a decadent aesthete, a lecher, a liar, a libertine, queer, a wife beater, an alcoholic, a drug addict, a plagiarist, a wannabe robber baron; an unpractical pragmatist with suspect metaphysics.

In 1891 Peirce, the first meteorologist to use a wavelength of light as a unit of measure and the inventor of the quincuncial projection of two spheres, was forced to resign from the United States Coast and Geodetic Survey, where among other things he had been in charge of gravity and pendulum research for 20 years. According to Beverley S. Kent's *Charles S. Peirce: Logic and the Classification of the Sciences*, the U.S. Coast Survey's international reputation as America's premier scientific institution was largely indebted to his genius.

It is more than likely that Peirce lost his academic position and his government appointment primarily because the lecturer in logic from a privileged upper-class background (mother—Sarah Hunt Mills, the daughter of Senator Elijah Hunt Mills ((Daniel Webster occupied Mills' senate seat when he retired)), father—Benjamin Peirce, founder of the Harvard Observatory, one of 50 incorporators of the American Association for the Advancement of Science, an organizer of the Smithsonian Institution, distinguished professor of mathematics at Harvard, considered America's premier (((if eccentric))) 19th-century mathematician, brothers—James Mills Peirce, professor of mathematics and dean of the graduate faculty at Harvard, Herbert Henry

Davis Peirce, distinguished foreign service career) flouted conventions of genteel scholarly decorum among the American learned by openly living with a European woman of uncertain background at the same time he was married to (although separated from) his first (recent rumor says second) wife, Harriet Melusina (Zina) Fay Peirce. Zina, also from a prominent New England family, was an influential feminist political organizer in Boston and Cambridge circles. She left him for undisclosed reasons in 1878 after 14 years of marriage. If Peirce had kept this love affair quiet it might have been tolerated in the academy and the Survey, but in 1881 he began divorce proceedings against his first wife for desertion. In 1883, only two days after their divorce was finalized, he married again. In Cambridge, Boston, and Baltimore Zina's public, unorganized "desertion" was also considered a breach of decorum. Unable to reinstate herself in polite circles (even as a radical feminist bluestocking) she moved to New York and Chicago, where she earned a meager living by managing boardinghouses, continued to write magazine articles, edited an edition of her sister Amy's letters, titled *Music Study in Germany*, and suffered increasingly from heart trouble and attacks of depression. Over the next 40 years she laboriously revised her now forgotten novel, *New York: A Symphonic Study,* published in 1918. I haven't been able to find a copy.

MS 1640: Juliette de Portalès from her friend and devoted servitor C.S. Peirce. [Fragment from the flyleaf of a German, French, English Dictionary, n. d.]

She might have been 17 or 19 years old. She might have been teaching him German. Elizabeth Walther (*Charles Sanders Peirce: Leben und Werk*, 1989) thinks Peirce might have met the enigmatic "Mme Pourtalai" during 1876 when he was in Berlin doing pendulum research for the Geodetic Survey. Following a trail of surnames through genealogical records in Germany, France, and Switzerland, Walther has discovered hints, rumors, embellishments, contradictions, erasures, negations, fictions. On the marriage certificate in the New York City Bureau of Records, April 26, 1883, Juliette Pourtalai's maiden name is given as Juliette Annette Froissy of

Washington, D.C., daughter of August Froissy and Rose [E]yem. The marriage to Peirce is listed as her second. She might have been the wife of a certain Pourtalai who had no first name, but there is no certificate from this former union, if there was one. Either the man was dead when she left Europe, or they were separated, or he never existed. An entry in one of Peirce's notebooks in Juliette's hand refers to "La Duchesse de Parme à Wartegg ma soeur." In another she listed places where she spent Christmas holidays in her youth. Some were spent in Nancy, apparently before her mother died. Archives in Nancy show no Froissys and no Count Pourtalai. Tracking the name Juliette Annette de Portalès, Walther was able to turn up an Anna Ada von Portalès (from a French family with a Swiss branch), the first child of Jacques Alfred von Portalès and his second wife, Sophie von Thielau, born July 28, 1857. But Anna Ada died April 17, 1889. Walther assures us it was not unusual for members of the German aristocracy to declare someone dead in order to disinherit them.

Babel wants a scourge for its wild

green grassblades not seeing me

Whatever Juliette's age or her surname the couple made sure it remained a secret. Joseph Brent (*Charles Sanders Peirce: A Life*, 1993) says that in the papers of Mary Eno Pinchot and her son, Governor Gifford Pinchot, there is correspondence and information concerning the Peirces, but even here all references to Juliette's identity have been removed. Mary Eno's daughter-in-law, Cornelia Bryce Pinchot, somewhat nastily hinted to someone that (among other possibilities) Juliette-Anna-Ada may have been one of a small group of "filles de joie" forced into exile by the French Third Republic for political reasons.

In 1936, shortly after her death, the younger Henry James (William James' son, not his brother) remembered Juliette telling Alice (William James' wife, not his sister) that after she arrived in New York in 1876 she lived at the Hotel Brevoort (the first house the James family occupied in New York City during the 1840s, at Fifth Avenue between Eighth and Ninth Streets, had been knocked down with some others to make way for the hotel). According to Brent, the Brevoort catered to the wealthy, titled, and socially important, and Peirce was well known by the staff. According to James, Juliette shyly stayed in her room until one evening the manager told her there was to be a reception, a party or a ball, and as he knew the hosts, he arranged to have her properly introduced as a guest. Juliette told Alice that this was where and when she met her future husband. The third Henry James cautioned Henry S. Leonard, who had written to him regarding the papers being collected at Harvard, against putting any information he might have to offer concerning Juliette's origin into print: "after all, it is Peirce, not Mrs. Peirce you are writing about and so far as he is concerned her importance consists not of where she came from or what she was before he married her, but of what she did for them after they were married." Nevertheless he felt obliged to add: "Mrs. Peirce's habit of concealing all names when she alluded to or told about her past is what makes everything so blind and dubious. . . .There is enough here to lay the foundations for a mystery story."

Joseph Brent portrays his eccentric subject as a manic-depressive, alcoholic, drug-addicted, debauched, debauching, Baudelairean dandy; difficult, but a genius. He blames the American mathematician-logician-philosopher's devotion to Juliette on the questionable influence of French *fin-de-siècle* poets and novelists. After all Peirce, a Francophile, was in Paris, where he presented a report of his discoveries on pendulum research at a meeting of the Permanent Commission of the International Geodetic Association during the turbulent autumn of 1875.

INDEX : 413

Kenneth Laine Ketner presents his theory as to Juliette-Fabiola's genealogy in *His Glassy Essence: An Autobiography of Charles Sanders Peirce*, (1998). (Father—Adolphe Fourier de Bacourt, a distinguished French monarchist diplomat well known in French and German circles, and as the French ambassador to Washington during 1840-42, acquainted with Benjamin Peirce, George Bancroft, and other cosmopolitan American scholars, politicians, and ambassadors ((Fabiola was illegitimate)). Mother—famous Gypsy flamenco dancer and singer of *cante jondo*, or "deep song," a music unique to the *Gitanos* of Andalusia). Over the caption *"Madame de Lopez / Would you care to see her photograph?"* Ketner supplies the portrait of an exceedingly grim middle-aged woman dressed in what appears to be mourning. Her left hand clutches at her skirt as if she were on the verge of running away or had just been caught in the act. In the act of *what*, who can say? Her right hand grips what or may not be a deck of playing cards protruding from the end of an elaborately studded, casket-shaped box probably intended for jewelry. When Juliette-Fabiola met Peirce at the Brevoort House (the Charles Sanders Peirce Professor of Philosophy at Texas Tech University and director of its Institute for Studies in Pragmaticism says it was a Christmas costume party and that Benjamin Peirce, who may have been acting as one of her several elite guardians, introduced her to his son) she was a sickly 19-year-old Romany orphan living in an apartment off Washington Square, under the care of her duenna or governess, the Marquise de Chambrun. You will have to read *His Glassy Essence* to learn how Ketner reaches this compelling conclusion. It seems to be largely based on Victor Lenzen's "Babcourt hypothesis," written for Max H. Fisch in 1973. Lenzen suggests she may have been a Gypsy, then changes his mind. In 1966, Charles Gassman, the Peirces' close neighbor, told Fisch that Gypsies were often in the Milford area, and as Juliette was friendly with them, he believed she might have been one herself. Ketner cites the pack of cards she kept encased in an inlaid box and may have used to tell fortunes and a letter to Charles from Wendell Phillips Garrison, the editor of *The Nation*, after having visited the couple in 1902: "My late lamented friend Dean Sage who loved all outdoors and was a great Booravian [George Henry Borrow, former hack writer, traveling hedge-smith, and author of *Lavrengo* and its sequel, *The Romany Rye,* among other popular accounts of works about the Romany world of Great Britain and Spain] went daft on the gipsies who haunted Albany for a time. As for fortune telling your wife did me up brown on your porch one day, with tales of deception & perhaps matrimony which I did not take down in shorthand. I have more respect for palmistry than for cards. . . ."

"There was nothing that Borrow strove against with more energy than the curious impulse, which he seems to have shared with Dr. Johnson, to touch the objects along his path in order to save himself from the evil chance. Walking through Richmond Park with the present writer he would step out of his way to touch a tree." In the article he contributed to the eleventh edition of *The Encyclopaedia Britannica* Theodore Watts-Dunton cautions readers against assuming George Borrow never created a character. Even if originals in his accounts seem easily recognizable, "the man who 'touched' to avert the evil chance has so many of Borrow's own eccentricities it could be called a portrait of himself." Rumor is a story passing from one person to one person without an original authorized relation. For Peirce sentiment comes from the heart, it must also be feigned. Demosthenes with his mouthful of pebbles had to talk without choking himself or allowing the pebbles to drop from his mouth. Verbal reverberations keep us safe, that is their interest. Emerson shows in the essay he titled "The Poet" how smallest things can serve for symbols, how every relation is picture-language. "Bare lists of words are found suggestive, to an imaginative and excited mind; as it is related of Lord Chatham, that he was accustomed to read in Bailey's Dictionary, when he was preparing to speak in Parliament." "If my name is a terror to evil doers," Noah Webster is rumored to have said to someone, "mention it."

In poetry all things seem to touch so they are.

After their marriage the Peirces lived in Manhattan. Juliette spoke French and German fluently, taught music and French, and was an accomplished pianist. Private theatricals were popular; she became a noted amateur actress and took singing lessons. She owned some valuable jewelry and received about 18,000 francs as a pension from somewhere. One reason the couple gave for hiding her identity was that if she didn't keep it a secret the payments would stop. Gypsies had been subjected to suspicion and penalties, hounded and persecuted throughout Western Europe: if she was half Romany, there would have been good reason never to trust anyone. They both enjoyed card tricks, word games, fortune-telling, charades. He drew a cartoon of her as "the bourgeoise Athena." Together they translated and performed in *Medea*.

MS 1572: A gentleman of reputation in science and philosophy (member of the U.S. Academy of Sciences) highly successful as a teacher (especially of those who are backward) will receive into his house in new York, and instruct, without the aid of accomplished assistants, in all or many branches, three or four strictly select ^{highly} pupils young gentlemen, extending some peculiar ~~opportunities~~ advantages for cultivation.

Drama of community never reached.

Phenomenology asks what are the elements of appearance. In my nature (cross out with) it is a sort of instinct toward (slash to) a solid (cross out visible) instinctive attraction for living facts. Microreproduction gives the trace of someone or something. Pens are noisy pencils quiet. What is the secret nature of fact? What is the fact that is present to you now? Between the law of the market and the law of exchange handwriting as noise cannot be enacted. Let y be y you cannot gasp at blue. On the one hand academic and antiquarian tendencies with lattice work in open gables on the other, Indianapolis. For most architects print modifications are silent. When I read an authorized edited Collected Work I read against original antiredness what ought to be seen, <u>generally</u>. Peirce calls secondness all naked feeling and raw life. Originality is in being such as thus this being <u>is</u>.

At that time] at time

Four years after his dismissal from Johns Hopkins, the couple pooled some money recently inherited from somewhere, and for one thousand dollars they acquired Thomas Quick's 140-acre farm on the western bank of the Delaware River ("the wildest county of the Northern States") two and a half miles from Milford, Pike County, Pennsylvania, seven miles below Port

Jervis, New York. They covered the outer walls of Quick's original farmhouse with shingles in the then fashionable New England "summer cottage" style and added floors and rooms, including a library for his large book collection. Max Fisch says the Peirces probably called their property "Arisbe" after a city in Troas, the ancient colony of Miletus, the home of the early Greek philosophers, Thales, Anaximander, and Anaximenes, who first searched for the Archē, the Principle, the first of things. I think Peirce named the house for Homer's "brilliant" or "shining" Arisbe.

Arisbe mark of mortality.

> Next *Teuthras'* Son distain'd the Sands with Blood,
> *Axylus*, hospitable, rich and good:
> In fair *Arisba's* Walls (his native Place)
> He held his Seat; a Friend to Human Race.
> Fast by the Road, his ever-open Door
> Oblig'd the Wealthy, and reliev'd the Poor.
> To stern *Tydides* now he falls a Prey,
> No Friend to guard him in the dreadful Day!
> Breathless the good Man fell, and by his side
> His faithful Servant, old *Calesius* dy'd. [*Iliad*, VI.15–24]

Alexander Pope was 25 when in spring 1714 economic necessity pushed him to begin the ambitious project of translating Homer into up-to-date English. As Roman Catholics he and his parents were unable to invest money easily, and their annuities from French *rentes* they depended on were in danger of default. The translation was to be published by subscription in the manner of Dryden's *Virgil*. Proposals were issued, the reaction was enthusiastic; 652 sets were reserved in advance. King George I and the Prince of Wales were among the subscribers. Only when he was sure of making a profit did Pope begin this work that for the next five years became his obsession. The first volume, containing the first four volumes of the *Iliad of Homer,* with a Preface, Essay, and Observations, printed by W. Bowyer for Bernard Lintot between the Temple-Gates, was delivered to subscribers in 1715 and established his reputation.

JOSEPH ADDISON: Reading the *Iliad* is like traveling through a Country uninhabited, where the Fancy is entertained with a thousand Savage Prospects of vast Desarts, wide uncultivated Marshes, huge Forests, misshapen Rocks and Precipices. On the contrary, the *Aeneid* is like a well ordered garden—

Roman Catholics in England weren't allowed to own property, but the money Pope earned allowed him lease a country villa near London. Here "The Hermit of Twickenham," or "Twitnam" as he preferred to call it, practiced elaborate landscape gardening, constructed his fantastic grotto, and received a constant stream of brilliant visitors, including John Arbuthnot, Lady Mary Wortley Montagu, John Gray, Lord Bolingbroke, Sarah Duchess of Marlborough, Bishop Atterbury, Jonathan Swift, even Voltaire. The much celebrated house and grounds have been associated with the poet-philosopher's name ever since.

Can a name be a prediction?

In Book XII Asios leaves Arisbe and is swallowed by dark-named Destiny. In Book XXI, Lykaon, a bastard son of Priam, captured by Achilles in an earlier struggle, is sold into slavery and shipped to Lemnos fortress until Eëtion out of Imbros pays a princely ransom for the captive and sends him to Arisbe's shining walls. There he is well treated until he foolishly escapes. After many difficulties Lykaon returns to Ilion where he joins his half brother Hector's army. Not for long. Twelve days later Achilles runs across him again by accident. Time (take Zeno's flying arrow) sets out in a past we place ourselves in. If the present is connected to the past by a series of infinitesmal steps (The Law of Mind) a past cannot be wholly past.

Lykaon sits back and spreads his arms wide
Achilles catches him by the foot and slings him in the river Scamander
     to drift
Xanthus chief river of the Trojan plain free blossoming meadows
     and murmuring waters of Scamander

Charles and Juliette Peirce find themselves owning property in order to secure a bourgeois existence. The house fronts on the old Milford Road, which follows the contour of the Delaware River from Port Jervis to Milford. The scenery and delightful summer climate have made the nearby Delaware Water Gap a delightful summer resort.

ALEXANDER POPE: Consult the Genius of the Place in all;
That tells the Waters or to rise or fall,
Or helps th'ambitious Hill the Heav'ns to scale—

MS 1611: He resides at his wife's country seat 'Arisbe,' near Milford, Pa., where he has a free school of philosophy, furnishing remunerative employment to such students as desire it. He also exercises the professions of chemist and engineer.

We are almost here but in a false position. There is no artificial grotto with an aquatic effect (plates of looking glass in an obscure part of the roof and sides of the cave, every object multiplied), no busts of Homer and Virgil to stimulate a visitor's thought. The picturesque in its late American stage is awkward and cut up. Something is wrong with the scale. Where are the visitors?

Arisbe imagined as a business transaction. The free school never materializes. The end of the Survey salary is shocking. Staring it in the face the material the unreal real thing that is in money enters into language by determining it. Recklessly they acquire more land, apple and nut orchards, a slate quarry. Both of them are very nervous very often very ill.

An authentic modern tragedy if we think of gold as being money.

A capitalist who loses everything is hurled headlong into the enormous wave of a money-fed river.

Forced to earn their support on what he could gain by various temporary means, Peirce produced an extraordinary number and variety of book reviews and essays (often anonymously) for a variety of journals, including *The Nation*, *The Monist*, and *Popular Science Monthly*. He gave occasional lectures, tutored students privately, worked on translations from the French and the German, collaborated on various encyclopedias and dictionaries (he composed most of the definitions on logic, mathematics, mechanics, astronomy, astrology, weights, measures, and all words relating to universities for W. D. Whitney's *Century Dictionary* and most of the articles on logic for J.M. Baldwin's the *Dictionary of Philosophy and Psychology*), served as a consulting chemical engineer for the St. Lawrence Power Company, gave lessons in elocution to Episcopal ministers, developed an invention for electrolytic bleaching, concocted a "Genuine Imitation/Cologne Water," joined well-heeled fellow members of the Century Club in New York in a venture to produce cheap domestic lighting from acetylene gas with a generator he invented and patented. But the national economic collapse during the 1890s left him bankrupt. Even the Century Club expelled him around 1898. After 1900 Peirce gave up trying to earn his living either by teaching or by science pure and applied and became the first American to list his profession as that of logician: a "bucolic logician," as he put it.

MS 1613: **Occupation**, Digestion psycho- and physio-logical.
Positions or Offices held since leaving the University, with dates,
Was once on the Commission to Examine the Mints
  Gave lectures at Bryn Mahr (I forget how to spell it)
    The rest weren't worth a fig, far less a date
Membership in Scientific or other learned Societies, Have been an Honorary Member of the Athenaeum Club in London and the Garde Voltaire (I am not at all sure of remembering the name) in Paris.
  I don't amount to a row of pins (according to any such more or <u>any</u> mode of estimation) The distinctions of which I am proudest is the devotion of friends, especially my wife & several women who I have never seen and probably never shall see.

While outlining the Pragmatic Principle in the *North American Review,*

October (1871), he first coined the term *pragmatism,* but it went unrecognized or unacknowledged until William James publicly used the word in a lecture at Berkeley in 1898, titled "Philosophical Conceptions and Practical Results." James said he was presenting "the principle of Peirce, the principle of pragmatism." Their ideas on the definition and principle were never identical. In 1903, after attending Peirce's Lowell Lectures, James referred to the current thought of his friend as "—flashes of light relieved against Cimmerian darkness." In 1905, Peirce, in a paper titled "What Pragmatism Is," announced the birth of the word pragmat<u>ic</u>ism, a name "which is ugly enough to keep it safe from kidnappers."

How are ideals maintained in the long story of responsibility? Secret.

The genteel American tradition is not to kill an original: we only remove the embarrassment.

MS 1611: **Honors Conferred**, Never any, nor any encouragement or aid of any kind or description in my life work, excepting a splendid series of magnificent promises.

Chief Subject of Research, Logic.

Where Chiefly Published, Not published except in slight fragments. See Schröeder's Logik.

Researches in Progress, In logic will continue as long as I retain my faculties & can afford pen and ink.

For the latter third of his life this philosopher's philosopher who once yearned to be hired as a professor *somewhere* drew and wrote (according to his own calculations) over 2,000 words, diagrams, algebraic formulas and/or existential graphs a day. His unpublished writings (including his correspondence) come to more than 100,000 pages.

Perhaps Peirce banished himself for logic's sake.

Juliette remains exactly who she never says she is she already burned her boats.

MS 1644: The robberies which have been going on at Arisbe Park, the large house of Madame Juliette Peirce on the Milford road, have reached a stage where drastic action is being sought. Sporadic burglaries and pettty thieveries have annoyed Mme. Peirce for several years, despite attempts to stop them and have frequently reached a stage where this talented lady, the widow of Charles Sanders Peirce the famous scientist, fears for her life.

In speaking of the recent robberies Mme. Peirce states that a very valuable ermine coat, with costly lining was stolen and as it represented a large amount of money and as well was valued for its usefulness, she feels its loss keenly. [THE MILFORD DISPATCH: *Mme. Peirce's home robbed of valuables.*]

Each of the 38 reels in the microfilm edition has the same brief preface far more brightly lit than the photocopied body:

> This microfilm prepared during the years 1963-1966 with the cooperation of the Houghton Library and the Photographic Service of the Harvard University Library, includes all of the Peirce papers in the custody of the Harvard Department of Philosophy except a certain body of correspondence, personal and professional. It includes drafts of some but not all of Peirce's published writings, for many of which no manuscripts are extant. The papers here reproduced were for the most part acquired from Peirce's widow in the winter of 1914-15, less than a year after his death.

The arrangers, cataloguers, editors, and custodians don't give Juliette's name, nor do they tell us the Department of Philosophy probably paid her at the most five hundred dollars for the lot. She had tried unsuccessfully to interest Yale University in taking on Arisbe, possibly as a memorial to her husband, but got no response. After her death Gifford Pinchot's lawyer wrote to Yale, Harvard, and Columbia to ask if they were interested in acquiring Peirce's remaining books, papers, and scientific instruments. They weren't.

MS 1644: Mrs. Juliette Pierce has donated to the Milford Fire Depart. $20. from the $45. she netted the past summer telling fortunes. The balance has been given for various purposes. Mrs. Peirce was sorry the goal she aspired to was not reached but periodic attacks of bronchitis have precluded giving as much time as usual to fortune telling. [THE MILFORD DISPATCH.]

Between 1931 and 1935 Harvard published the first six volumes of what was hopefully called *The Collected Papers of Charles Sanders Peirce*. The general plan was for ten volumes, but money ran out after volume six. All the work for this edition was accomplished by a junior instructor and a graduate student volunteer. While the secondary scholarship on Peirce's work was steadily growing, Arisbe had no plumbing and no heat. Only two rooms remained furnished. Juliette lived in one of them alone with her husband's portrait, his unwanted scientific equipment, the remains of his book collection, other memorabilia (including his ashes in a silver urn), and a set of china. She died in October 1935, under "circumstances not suitable to sustain life or dignify death," according to the doctor who attended her. Trees and lilac bushes around the house had grown so high it was invisible from the road only 50 feet away. The property was left empty for two years until it was auctioned in 1936 for $3,600. Arisbe's new owners lit a bonfire in the neglected front garden and burned whatever relics burglars hadn't already carried off.

This was before the age of tag sales.

THOMAS WENTWORTH HIGGINSON: Look to the physical aspect of your manuscript, and prepare your page so neatly that it shall allure instead of repelling. Use good pens, black ink, nice white paper and plenty of it. Do not emulate "paper-sparing Pope," whose chaotic manuscript of the "Iliad," written chiefly on the backs of letters, still remains in the British Museum. If your document be slovenly, the presumption is that its literary execution is the same, Pope to the contrary, notwithstanding. ["Advice to a young Contributor," *Atlantic Monthly*, April, 1862.]

On the fifteenth of April 1862, Emily Dickinson sent a first letter to her future editor, probably in response to his "Advice." She enclosed four poems, including "We play at Paste—,"and a separate card bearing her name.

Lewis Mumford noted in *The Brown Decades: A Study of the Arts in America 1865-1895* (1931) that the publication of Peirce's manuscripts had lagged for lack of a few thousand dollars to guarantee the initial expenses of his "Collected Works" and compared the situation to the concealment of Emily Dickinson's manuscripts by overzealous guardians. Martin Gardner wondered in *Logical Machines and Diagrams* (1982) if Peirce harbored unconscious compulsions toward cloudy writing that would enable him to complain later of his critics' inability to understand him. In "Communication, Semiotic Continuity, and The Margins of the Peircian Text" (1997), Mary Keeler and Christian Kloesel tell us the secondary literature on Peirce demonstrates that only the hardiest scholars have made use of his manuscripts and even then only by way of photocopies, and that his work is unpublishable in print form. I wonder why manuscripts are so underestimated in all academic disciplines, including science, mathematics, linguistics, semiology. It's 1999

> I will print you a syllabus
>
> Continuity probability even
>
> the predictability of drift

1910 Sep 13   It is my duty to investigate Modality more closely

A certain existing man might be attacked without defending himself

A person may dream that Theodore Roosevelt attacks him

———— dream

Field of may-be   T. R.

the dream is real

attacks

a person has adream

MS 1644:

(iii) Designated page "Husband's Demise April 18"

Full name Charles Sanders Peirce

One of our last conversation, I remember started with him that he could not recover physically by hard mentale work & in refusing to let him have more paper to write, but when he complained his pains were so great & writing would easing his pains, then I complied. The doctor had left opiats to aliviate his great suffering but he refused to take. In handing me his last writings in stating my best is finished & will make a revolution in science, life will be easy for you and we are gone to travell again. Then he requested me to pick him out a book of Dickens to relax from hard work at random I handed him *Dombey* & he remarked when finished I reading that it was the only book of Dickens he knew not ending so gloomy. I was hopefull that he would recover again he also predicted that great war again.

I was most hopeful he would

Constraint is a secondness

swimming out to sea Europe

Between an interpretant and

its object in playspace the

heart's free interim Macbeth's

crude sacrilege deeper even

Spent those last years not

writing his paper on misery

I remember all the time now

remember the brood the fret

Iliadic heroism another situation

of unstable identity Polydorus

comes onstage he has appeared

in a dream to Hecuba the outer

covering of his body remnant of

Cloth wrung out soft wool left stray

Hecuba and chorus address the

shield as tomb so memory does

wash over holy ablution water

Change wounds Hector tumbles

in the dust but the wife of Hector

has not heard she is inside what

fate metes out this and this dactyl

Achilles has come by land Ilios

Chorus of Thessalonian women

rush from beyond the famous land

of evening your torches blazing

Cold rushes little feet acting out

Let him down gently no don't

ask who I am it is still night and

invading armies don't you see

elements of her hurt her child

enters the world suffused with

his fate O my Thetis unchecked cry

the hidden fate of things to be

If you were human you would

seize spear and sword to rout

ruin lust lechery *humanum est*

errare Patroclus' armor three times

he charges with the force of a

running war god brute Apollo

Strip away Patroclus' armor

Achilles-Patroclus' helmet

crusted in horsehair off too

But the ink is scarcely dry

Ramping brute force know

Hector was the third slayer

→ Actuality is something brute

Unspelled Firstness is first

Move the shuttle-thread give

ghostly instruction ferryman

- In context of the Iliad
- Tells story of a specific scene
- about Patroclus' death
- Is like a list

O patiently people being

blown to bits one hand

clutching bandages next

bit proverb and byword

Through mined copyhold

we are all here Realism

Is hidden escape possible

One mind as what-is-not

THE LEISURE OF
THE THEORY CLASS

with best regards
from ACSwinburne

No. 115 George Meredith's

fountain pen given to

E.D. Brooks on a visit

to Flint Cottage shortly

before his death by his

nurse Miss A. Nichol no

Miss Nichol did not kill

Meredith to be plausible

it might have been a pen

collector a Dickens pen

another Brooks acquisition

Fantastic lyric material

His first wife was the

first daughter of Thomas

Love Peacock the author

for whose writings Mr.

Meredith always professed

most sincere admiration

Husband and wife lived

apart (*Modern Love*) she

had wandered about for

some time after running

off with the artist who

painted Peacock's portrait

Now in *Memories* out of

earshot her expression

on a sheet of white paper

We pace and want even if

two drops of water differ

from one another can we

saying yours never not look

Not look back oh I would

What shall we say person

to person I see the side-lie

We went side by side but

Side-lie this is my breast

In 1885 in *Memories* he

loved old Dr. Gordon who

once lived in Weimer and

for a time had known Goethe

Out of earshot reading

of life when speaking of

seeing by empathy clasp

silhouette taken by Sir John

Butcher, Bart., K.C., M.P.

Little sketch *Ideal-Real*

GEORGE MEREDITH

Silhouette taken by Sir John Butcher, Bart.,
K.C., M.P., in 1885.

Frontispiece

"Peacock's wife became mad

so there was a family taint—"

No tombstone has been placed

over the place where I lie to the

left near the top of the main path

In the churchyard at Weybridge

Mary Ellen Meredith died alone

Remorse is felt in *Modern Love*

Lost reality links grisly humor

in *The Amazing Marriage* to an

analytic philosopher who represents

the common spirit small causes

nothing to rouse no fatal person

Meredith is never tired of talking

as they wheel him in his garden

I talked with him about

the writings of Fiona

Macleod he told me he

knew Fiona Macleod was

really William Sharp

but he sincerely hoped

Mr. Sharp would never

know he had penetrated

the mystery pseudonym

He hated being exploited

for his own "great name"

other stories about how

they were received

and shown about by

Meredith's last nurse

his last pencil how she

arranged for Brooks

to meet Arthur Symons

of fringe prominence

in the aesthetic Nineties

when he was in England

gathering up pens

of the famous dead

In 1900 Swinburne who died

in 1909 just a month before

Meredith (he had been living

a cloistered life at 2 The Pines

in Putney) told Arthur Symons

he no longer wished to write

on imperial or patriotic subjects

—*other archaic Greek messages*

indiscoverable lands all law

torn up nothing praiseworthy—

Before the beginning of years

~~And the~~ ~~to plait~~ of ~~wrinkles~~
And the ~~kindling~~ of the stars

In the ~~state~~ ~~far lands~~ of the sky

There arose up

Strength without hands to fight;
~~Love with tears~~ ~~for breath~~
~~Love the shadow~~ ~~And love that~~ Love that endures for a breath;

Night the shadow of light,
And life the shadow of death.

The heart of a man

Before the beginning of years

There came to the making of man

~~Grief~~ with a gift of tears;

Time with a glass that ran;

Pleasure with pain for leaven;

Summer with flowers that fell;

~~The days~~ ~~that are~~ ~~lent in~~ heaven

Remembrance fallen from heaven

And madness risen from hell;

And the high gods took in their hands

~~Earth to make~~ ever withal

Fire, and the falling of tears,

a measure of ~~sliding~~ sands

And salt of the sea;

~~These measures~~ ~~stole~~ from under the feet of the years;

And froth & drift of the sea;

And dust ~~of the~~ coloring earth;

And ~~shadows~~ bodies of things to be

In the houses of death and of birth;

And wrought with weeping and laughter

And ~~clothes~~ fashioned with loathing and love

And ~~dust~~ with life before and after

With the ~~division~~ of times thereafter

~~down~~ light

And ~~grief~~ ~~night~~ beneath & above

Mr. Watts-Dunton pulls

from Swinburne's desk

an object to be loved

above all others it

signifies tenacity as

he sat home in Putney

as he had written <u>here</u>

Watts-Dunton's faith

in habit is not Brooks'

item 184 because nerve-

fossils show relation

is singular singular a

sign for some one you

cannot put 2 and 2 to

gether no not even a

wielder of Ockham's razor

Let us go hence, my songs; she will not hear.
Let us go hence together without fear.
Keep silence now, for singing-time is over,
And over all old things & all things dear.
She loves not you nor me as all we love her:
Yea though we sang ~~all~~ as angels in her ear,
        she would not hear.
Let us ~~turn~~ rise up ~~& sleep~~ part; she will not know.
Let us go sea-ward as the great winds go,
Full of ~~sand~~ blown sand & foam; what help is here!
There is no help, for all these things are ~~because we together so~~
~~Help us for her sake from evil cheer~~
And all the world is bitter ~~too~~ as a tear.
And how ~~we love her~~ these things are, ~~she~~ ye strove to show,
        she would not know.

Let us go home & hence; she will not weep.
~~why should we~~ ~~now~~ ~~what have but thorns to reap?~~
For ~~this~~ fair sea-fields where ~~in~~ the foam flowers grow,
~~Reap~~ no thorns forth; ~~the~~ red they ~~take~~ they keep,
And ~~over it the~~
~~I love our ~~ ~~red about~~ ~~it waved~~
~~Leave lost her~~ ~~to give grief to ~~all they gave him~~
~~We gave love all~~ ~~day & days~~ to keep
No need of tears ~~for~~ songs now; shall ~~these~~ float
For love's sake ~~the~~ days that
We ~~gave~~ love many dreams & days to keep
~~flowers to ~~ ~~without scent~~ & fruits that ~~will not grow~~
And he hath given ~~grow them~~ ~~sorrow~~ ~~& her half reap,~~
~~Neither he hath given to sorrow, ~~nor~~ her half reap,~~
~~or~~ saying, ~~& If~~ thou wilt thrust in thy sickle & reap.
All is reaped now; no grass is ~~left~~ ~~to ~~ now
And ~~we~~ ~~that~~ ~~all we died~~ fell on sleep,
        she would not weep.

Silver age shaken authority

fevered ages quickly arrive

and the old royal family so

familiar to me that I seem in

reading to live the iron age

over am civil stranger foreign

Republic neither to be going

to be nor to be going not to

be a future determinately no

No the golden age of poetry

Peacock had no followers

he lived through nearly

thirty years of the Victorians

Among contemporary authors

he most enjoyed Dickens

and re-read him in his last

year "continually in fits

of laughter" Swinburne also

loved reading Dickens

aloud—Mrs. Skewton in her

bath chair *Dombey and Son*

Buckling his seat belt
the curator thought we
are in thought extreme
nominalism we've got to
frame another logic so
we will have the practist
where we want him flip
those leaves hastily to
a time Swinburne comes
storming into the shop
shrilly complaining over
something open to doubt
What are you driving at

—The Whippingham Papers

A bibliography of

Meredith contains nothing

so disturbing George

Meredith at Box Hill

offers hospitality to

more reputable friends

than either Augustus

Howell or Simeon Solomon

—1926 T. Earle Welby

C.S. Peirce is not the only

example other masterminds

knocked at academic portals

and were refused entry but

they are the obituaries a penalty

paid for safety for grammar

for scripture for Ockham time

and motion do not have the

same definition—*Commentary*

Davidson cracked the whip

of Aristotle we always

wound up with a quarrel

about space perception

We took a thin thread

half of the same paper

and by the sun's light

transumed religion in

the pale morning away

from prevalent fashion

No need to repeat here

particulars not dated by

his own reference to

earlier glosses even to

redaction of earlier

lectures our perceptions

somehow fail for failing

perceptual knowledge of

"pure experience" no two

"ideas" of future selves

One explicit knowledge

He worked over *Tristram*

in fits and starts

Love refrain of wind and

sea its intellectual

purpose in spirit *Tristram*

is ecstatic song if

printed and confined

Love's sail is black

Padding about in socks

"O God if there is a

God which there isn't

where are my damn boots"

The chair I appear to

see does not stand

for anything it knocks

at the portals of my

soul insistent for all

its silence as founder

Something being true

Turn over these pages

Husserl observes in a

marginal note "Better

to have written this

in reverse order"

The coming of Love

Rhona Boswell's Story

and other poems by

Theodore Watts-Dunton

author of *Aylwin*

[ALAMEIDA PUBLIC LIBRARY]

Afterwards the hero of

the novel confounded by

the hero of the poem

began to write criticism

If the book is to be opened

I must open it to open it

I must go get it if I am to

go get it I must walk if I

walk I must stand if I am

to stand I must rise if I am

to rise I had better put my

my foot down here is where

consciousness grows dim

Occamists frequently commit

mistakes Hume falls into

error it may be simple

error on my part I carry

the weight of my scissors

Mr. Brooks is a bibliophile

it doesn't matter to Hume

a practist must understand

being cut up by executors

A curator is a nit-picker

I can't find a signal-tree

What do you mean by a sign

There are realities

independent of thought

Evidence commentary scholia

Ransack thought-signs a

thousandth silhouette

P.S. (*Afterthought.*)

The store was dark

The curator knocked on glass

his Watts-Dunton shelf

"Whatever my thumb rests on

I shall take as having reference

to my work." His thumb hit the

words "What a work it is likely

to turn out! Let me begin it."

1846—Dickens went to Lausanne

he carried in his book-box

a copy of *Tristram Shandy*

G.W. Garrod calls Sterne's book

the *sors shandeana for Dombey*

Peacock was greatly shaken

by a fire breaking out in the

roof of his bedroom he was

carried to the library at the

other end of the house away

from more danger and water

A curate came to beg him to

move into one of the houses

in the neighborhood "By the

immortal Gods I will not move"

He would not leave his books

and lay ill for a few weeks

until he died 23 January 1866

To the sea calling on names of

Proteus the Nereids the rivers

lakes fields springs Limniads

Limoniads Ephydriads Oberon

All that is peripheral prefatory

The terra incognita of the not

proven that stretches between

the firm ground of the proved

and the void of the disproved

Bottom's other monopolylogue

early Hera precinct of Hera

knotted fillets on her wrist

tassels across her body she

is flanked by her peacocks

accompanied by Nemesis (her

peacocks are called *strouthoi*)

Typhon Styx Kronos Sleep

Guardian Nereids float over

Carrying this dedication leaf

to within our sphere of life

Thetis says she will go up

on land to see Achilles and

find out what sorrow has

befallen him she comes out

of the sea her sisters follow

she speaks only of herself

Why are Nereids forgotten

when she begins speaking

Nereids come and go without

an active part in anything

Blue Hill Plymouth Piscataqua

River returned by twilight to

this uninhabited room where

no one waits to welcome me

except old books—July 1870

Inveterate wanderer evidence

of something wrong a screw

loose when the class in Latin

Greek or whatever else called

Chauncey failed to hear "life"

A knot of us—Chauncey Wright

Nicholas St. John Green Francis E.

Abbot William James John Fiske

Oliver Wendell Holmes Jr. Chase

Joseph Bangs Warner among others

gathered to discuss metaphysical

questions force law fate Darwin—

I remember how angry people were

when a furniture dealer cut down

elms to build a store Cambridge

was a lovely old place at the time

Left a page here a page

there Wright's law and

he himself a name had he

escaped this King Arthur

after the fatal battle this

is the great King Arthur

He dreamed of flying or

floating in air owl-like

above the ground *terra*

incognita its voluptuousness

Elocutionists are at odds

as to whether there should

be a slight pause after the

subject of an assertion or

downright silence unless

an actual sheet is a surface

upon which any graph may

be scribed to the purpose

—Talking in his best vein

not about things but ideas

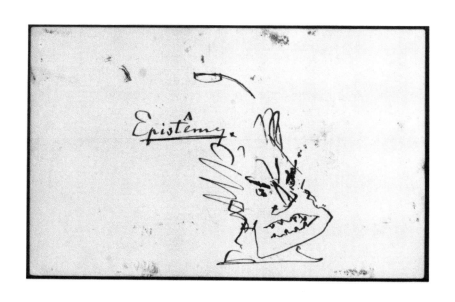

70

From 1860 on in nineteenth

century American colleges

philosophy was an apology

for Protestant Christianity

Thayer has pinned clippings

that identify the "professor

Sophocles" to whom Wright

referred as Professor Evangelinus

A. Sophocles full professor

of Greek at Harvard College

Half of the company

would try to portray

some abstract quality

Fear Courage Ambition

Love Conceit Hypocrisy

as a form of charade

as in dumb crambo

there is a danger in

over-obscurity what

happened through my

training danger might be

lessened if logical

analysis is an art

"We are dreadfully real, Mr. Carker,"

said Mrs. Skewton, "are we not?"

Dealings with the Firm of Dombey and Son:

Wholesale, Retail, and for Exportation

First published in book form in April 1848

—Charles Dickens

Schiller's essay in *Mind* Bain's

belief-doubt theory terminal note

to this running note what is the

assurance of good in the universe

in *Mr. Nightingale's Diary* Dickens

plays six different roles a lawyer

a waiter a gabbling old woman a

maniacally enthusiastic walker a

hypochondriac and a deaf sexton

Juliette Annette Froissy

Pourtalai (or de Portalès

said to be the widow of

a Count Portalai her true

surname is still unknown)

What I see is the image

or hidden correspondence

Sometimes she claims to be

a Hapsburg princess she

knew Kaiser Wilhelm II

(they were children together

her mysterious income

Her new first name if

it is she is Anna Ada

von Portalès born in

Laasow/Niederlausitz (then

Prussia) the first of

seven children on table

5 Genealogical Appendix

But Anna died April 17

1889 unmarried is there

ever absolute certainty

Peirce had no idea she

spoke Polish among half

a dozen other languages

Cold but bright

The little Blood boy

brought in our mail

14

St. Valentine's Day

Still snowing

Sunday Feb 15

Deep snow

Blood was in a

little while

Footprints outside

Sunday 22

About the coldest yet

Tuesday 24

I sat up all last night

Opened 4" box perique

Monday 2 March

Blizzard

C.O. Milford Pa. 1904

The way bleak north

presents itself here

as Heraclitean error

driving and driving

thought and austerity

nearer to lyricism

Often as black ice

Peirce left a blank

to fill in later in a

violent rupture of

nomenclature Euclid

What Greek geometer

does not want Heaven

out of touch with our

black earth hold on

Elements is occupied

with algebra itself

I do not know of any

other Peirce or Pierce

in the Milford vicinity

from Descartes to Hume

how utterly *Useless*

all metaphysicians are

What we said earlier

mere things the strata

or a "rule" in algebra

I might have called

it "practism" but

my dear Lady Welby

perfect accuracy of

thought is suspect

I doubt I shall ever

cross the water again

We say "type-written"

here something about

printer's copy modern telepathy

What I want to write

blurred in utmost

haste I call logic

to rhyme with metric

or optic very very

experiential ground

Always suspect a triad

Among these theses

are example ghosts

Now you see what

the word <u>real</u> means

After all we want

to get our thought

expressed in short

meter somehow but

I will write to you

when I can be more

definite by belief

I mean holding for true

Outside autography

body is my Body

C.S. Peirce "Arisbe"

Your "type" is better

ours sounds German

A copy many precursors

on my study mantlepiece

between listing numbers

by the Husserl Archives

1912 in dense shorthand

mostly in one stroke of

the Gabelsburger system

You take division's side

You and the Oxford thinkers

Certain things are mine

Why did someone erase the name

of the secret recipient of an

autograph inscription signed by

the famous author A.C. Swinburne

First in relation to a second

Thirdness—a customer upstairs

was passing through crisis in

The Cricket on the Hearth that

"Someone" was Swinburne himself

Duration flowing away

passes into emptiness

A pencil entry erased

to prevent recovery by

any infrared ultraviolet

low-level light image-

enhancing technique is

how not-now perceived

the past is perceived

"Before the mind"
What dogma disappeared
before any mind was
imaged and imagined

Manuscript section 3
"On The Constitution Of
Spirit" has its source
in the so-called H-folio
In 1928 after Husserl's
last pen touched the MS
it was set aside

To the denied Universe

we humans are already

something believed in

within belief in the

world in its first three

paragraphs the Sixth

Meditation by itself

Geist ("spirit") goes out

mostly at one stroke blue

Invisible he will not know

the hand and hand's field

Those annotations so often

cryptic as if the Middle Ages

breathed and moved again

From the Husserl-Archives

but not as Body after all

One of the redactors

calls Tristan David's

descendant his first

voyage Ireland avant

affiliation to reality

If suffering composes

psalms look out David

If verbal circularity

being to soul what eye

is according to half-

reading what will what

Andromache cry out in

winged words take up

the glittering reins it is

early morning the gates

are categories Predicate

placard postwar polyglot

Bare lists of words to be

thrown at the President

Milford semi-isolation

"The Kant of America"

Putney semi-isolation

"Shelley the second"

Mr. Wise collected the

scattered writing Gosse

furnished the necessary

critical Introduction

Faint line brown ink

image upper left corner

Tiny hand almost mirror

floating on a few blots

Where "entagled" <u>sic</u>

'h' correct were

Cancel sing here

Some ruin "beleif"

"we" ink "deramed"

poison vs. potion

"duble Isolt" Tristan

Peace thereafter

Rest fathom over

Rest oversea homage

Spread wing without

record windworn sail-

fable now you are

nothing no necessary

knowledge we know

Knowledge venom soft

Softly two kingdoms

The long wrangling

—I have tried to show

Shakespeare's probable

influence upon his "friend

of friends" It would have

been a mistake however

to cast the sonnets in

the same metrical mode

as Shakespeare's

Christmas 1898—T.W-D.

Achilles himself cannot wish

to slay himself for the wrong

he has done his alter-ego Hector

Hector disguised as Patroclus

Hector self-object of Achilles

Who by impersonating Achilles

will ever overtake the tortoise

Mirror-impulse ask Fortinbras

The portrait by Sandys

of a second wife hung alone

on the mantelpiece

There in his own chair

by the fire Mr. Meredith

Mr. Meredith himself

The second wife's piano

had been replaced

by a table used for meals

Mrs. Charles S. Peirce owns

articles of great historic

interest among them a pack

of playing cards which were

used with great success in

telling the fortunes of members

of the court retinue even of

Napoleon himself it is said

that Mlle LeNormand with these

cards predicted his downfall

The Misses Frost (corner

of Ridgeway and High)

ordered his books he

did not regard novels

as literature but life

in his long afterlife

at the Pines days he

lived with Watts well

after *The Triumph of Time*

She had come across

a bundle of notes on

"time-consciousness"

so described how she

and "the Master" put

the manuscript together

Scraps of notepaper

Refusing to settle into

stable *Husserliana*

Among Peacock's papers a
rough sketch for a grave-
stone was found on which
he had written Mary Ellen's
name and an inscription
in Greek "Earthly love is
soon forgetful / the heavenly
remembers always—"

Love changes besides he's
damned I cannot be at peace
perishing not to be heard of
Things that are not *are*

A nightingale sings in

secret language the bird

is betrayed when her love

song is made public in

secret language a poet's

public voice I bear the

Mary Ellen name in ambiguity

am I a ghost you know

Who was and was not

What we come to know

Who was and was not

We sing side by side

Slain life treads down tell

me stage love follows <u>if</u>

she wrapped up the bird

in a piece of silk took the

small betrayed nightingale

pledged she herself yes to

bargain for a blue thing or

forfeit architectonic all his

handwriting to me shows

logic of this poetic tradition

Actors are the usual three

Say of Hera she is

air but she did not

stoop toward it to

go under cover in

the main text took

the matter to heart

and died of it of

her realities crazy

air as a matter of

fact each holds to

its own I am to you

in a strict sense

a stationary state

Blind flight do we win
at last trusting to mad
strife in blindness not
holding to be mortal in
afterlife with arrows to
pierce dust and surf who
can discern or declare
What is due from guest
to host—*A Nympholept*

I will send you *Comedy and*
the Uses of the Comic Spirit

—Mary Ellen had been dead
a long time his preoccupation
was with medicine now he
could no longer be divided
between two sets of feelings

Academia wore Peirce

out long before

the massive literature

of Peirciana

Barrier of trees a

darkened wood *Evening*

retreating figure

Love needs a responding

love

He never could live within

his income

He contrived a hideout from

creditors in the attic

to which he would flee

drawing up the ladder

leading to it

He was meticulous

in his work

Writing and rewriting

He could never be relied upon

to do anything promptly

if ever

Gra glo gla skro shra schlo

skla

anuro annura anulo

angra angla astro ashla

wanuro wiskla

The Passing of a Master Mind

—*The Nation* May 14th 1914

One evening in the spring

of 1914 Theodore Watts-Dunton

(his mother's maiden name

by deed poll and hyphen)

quietly died in his sleep

he was resting on a sofa

near the last best photograph

of Swinburne (Photo: Poole,

Putney) Clara Watts-Dunton

didn't remarry Swinburne's

library became her bedroom

I have one terror resting-

place and bridge cross to

philosophy wavering line

What rule war imagery a

zeal skeleton we catch at

Legend those lost days our

policy by theft what lamp

They do not look to love

Do you understand what

our song is do you hope

to conquer night by song

Mr. Charles Sanders Peirce
introduced "practice" and
"practical" into philosophy
As when someone planning a
journey blind-eyed solitary
prepares a lamp and fastens
linen screens and the fine
linens from that moment end
with a question of fire in
flight the word "pragmatism"
spread pleading particulars

Husserl's *Nachlass* his

transcendental phenomenology

Cartesian Meditations

Appendixes to the main text

Fink's own copy of the

Sixth Meditation a massive

system the urgency of his

position in context of

the times then preparing

Nachlass for the future

Trench letters do get used

eventually for poetry you

long history of nihilism

Get ready to advance don't

everyone rattle camouflage

as if we are nothing only

company dive-bomb anxiety

A few persistent "islands"

of half-inaudible whispers

jabbing the radioman Lethe

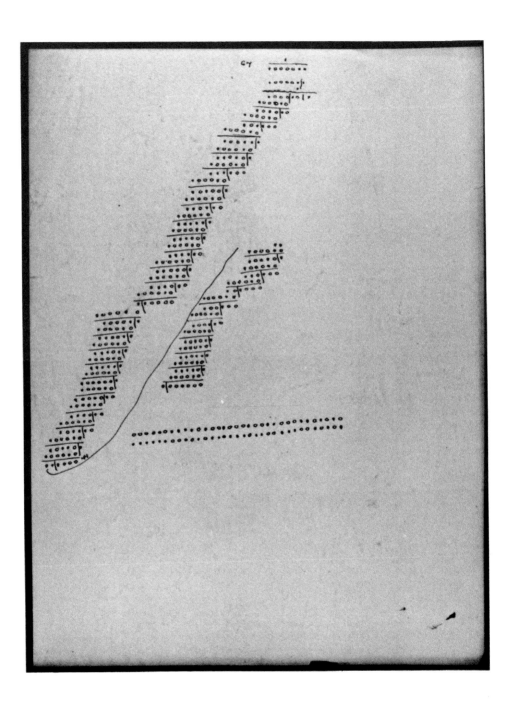

MS 1606: One of my earliest recollections is of hearing Emerson deliver his address on Nature and I think on that same day Longfellow's Psalm of Life was recited. So we were within hearing of the Transcendentalists, though not among them. I remember when I was a child going upon an hour's railway journey with Margaret Fuller, who had with her a book called the Imp in the Bottle.

117

GEORGE SANTAYANA: Seventy is a nice age. I suppose one is influenced without knowing it. . . . When I was young I was influenced by Percy.

BRUNO LIND: (blankly) Percy? *(Charles Peirce. I had never heard the name pronounced in that manner.)*

GEORGE SANTAYANA: Don't you know him, the pragmatist? Well, nobody could hire him. He was a drunkard. But when he was sober! I heard some of his lectures. I remember particularly an illustration he used—a thermometer. It's a dynamic symbol—anything telling you quantity. That of course fits in with my system. I distinguish between the dynamic side of nature and all the imaginative or symbolic side, which is ideas.

Please indifferent reader you

into whose hands this book

may fall without hope already

drawn to essays even with so

light a sketch of character life

No key or familiar footing in

respect to a private philology

no a priori philosophy before

we go free as fresh love half-

enchanted for finding out may

prove fallibilism to be fallible

Poet talking to reader
It's a message
Sense rides on the reader
knowing nothing before reading
the poem

On page 234 Brooks

pops up again as

"Mr. Edward Brooks

of Minneapolis" a

retroactive argument

for the negelected

God hypothesis lone-

lier than ruin in

Fechner's monograph

Exhausted certainty

after 1900 ink dis-

persed randomly has

some sort of order

It is a million-to-one

bet Brooks saw Item 115

in Dawson's catalogue

Forty Years in My Bookshop

was not the Mother Lode

he thought it would be

(Nominalist law is pre-

established by author)

but it set the Collector

on the right track "Now

break in now" he thought

I found in dreams a place of wind & flowers

Full of soft trees & colour of glad grass,

In midst whereof there was

A lady walking, clothed as summer is

Clothed by smooth hands of

    Scaped hills with faint woods loosely scarfed

    About them, ~~a grey ground~~, gap-toothed cleaps;

    Blind quinny heath against the dwarfed

      Blank powdered olive-cleaps.

~~The mouth was like that~~

~~Her lips were fashioned in such~~

    ~~Her mouth was~~

   ~~There was~~   ~~Love had~~ The bleak day's bloodless mouth of fight

      Gaped at the quest, gorge dolorous

      ~~There was~~ laid asleep upon her mouth

Sorrow had kissed her eyelids ~~alone~~ stiff Blackthorns its

The heavy rose curled upon her mouth two horns

    ~~Till the like a red~~ The whole world's sweetest one

Though the essay was never
completed only a rough draft
I can still see the room those
unmeant thoughts composed
in sleep now first printed on
four sides of double-octavo
sheet black-border notepaper
Never yours—Most sincerely
From the confines of poetry

Depressed by raw icy air
my nerves are by nature
of foggy climate nervous
the *twoness* of two hats
Nervous moving the hat
from side to side why not
either magic or science

Explosion of the theological
view thunder from dogma
Nervous moving the two
from side to side why not
have the relief of reading a
Greek tragedy

In 1898 Theodore Watts

("the foremost English

critic of literature

since Matthew Arnold"

—1910 *Harmsworth Encyclopedia*)

became Watts-Dunton

Within living memory

(—1971 Jean Overton Fuller

Swinburne; a biography)

Mr. Yglesias a skating

solicitor met Mrs. Watts-Dunton

who was also skating

Madame Peirce will give as

much time as possible for

her work in this city we

cannot count on a long stay

as she is wanted at other

places before summer is over

An adept at astrology she

has been engaged in doing

her work for philanthropy

RÜCKENFIGUR

Iseult stands at Tintagel

on the mid stairs between

light and dark symbolism

Does she stand for phonic

human overtone for outlaw

love the dread pull lothly

for weariness actual brute

predestined fact for phobic

falling no one talking too

Tintagel ruin of philosophy

here is known change here

is come crude change wave

wave determinist caparison

Your soul your separation

But the counterfeit Iseult

Iseult aux Blanches Mains

stands by the wall to listen

Phobic thought of openness

a soul also has two faces

Iseult's mother and double

Iseult the Queen later in *T*

Even *Tros* echoes Tristan's

infirmity through spurious

etymology the Tintagel of *Fo*

not the dead city of night

Wall in the element of Logic

here is a door and beyond

here is the sail she spies

Tristran Tristan Tristrant

Tristram Trystan Trystram

Tristrem Tristanz Drust

Drystan these names concoct

a little wreathe of victory

dreaming over the landscape

Tintagel font icon twilight

Grove bough dark wind cove

brine testimony Iseult salt

Iseut Isolde Ysolt Essyllt

bride of March Marc Mark in

the old French commentaries

your secret correspondence

Soft Iseut two Iseults one

The third of Tristan's overt

identities is a double one

his disguise as nightingale

in *Tros* then wild man in *Fo*

Level and beautiful La Blanche

Lande of disguise episodes

the nocturnal garden of *Tros*

Fo recalls the scene in Ovid

Orpheus grief stricken over

the loss of Eurydice sits by

the bank of a river seven days

I see Mark's shadow in water

Mark's moral right to Iseult

David's relationship to Saul

Lean on handrail river below

Sense of depth focus motion

of chaos in Schlegel only as

visual progress into depth its

harsh curb estrangement logic

Realism still exists is part

of the realist dual hypothesis

Dual on verso as one who has

obeyed acceleration velocity

killing frost regenerative thaw

you other rowing forward face

backward Hesperides messenger

into the pastness of landscape

inarticulate scrawl awash air

Insufferably pale the icy

limit pulls and pulls no

kindness free against you

Deep quietness never to be

gathered no blind threat

Assuredly I see division

can never be weighed once

pale anguish breathes free

to be unhallowed empty what

in thought or other sign

roof and lintel remember

Searching shall I know is

some sense deepest moment

What is and what appears

The way light is broken

To splinter color blue

the color of day yellow

near night the color of

passion red by morning

His name of grief being

red sound to sense sense

in place of the slaying

Tristram must be caught

Saw the mind otherwise

in thought or other sign

because we are not free

Saw the mind otherwise

Two thoughts in strife

Separation requires an

other quest for union

I use a white thread

half of the same paper

and in the sun's light

I place a lens so that

the sea reflects back

violet and blue making

rays easily more freely

your nativity and you

of light from that of

memory when eyelids close

so in dream sensation

Mind's trajected light

It is precision we have

to deal with we can pre-

scind space from color if

Thomas was only using a

metaphor and metaphysics

professes to be metaphor

There is a way back to the

misinterpretation of her

message TheseusTristan is

on the ship AegeusIseut

is a land watcher she is

a mastermind her frailty

turned to the light her

single vision twin soul half

Dilemma of dead loyalty

Mark's speeches are sham

Gottfried shows Tristan

only hunting for pleasure

Emerald jacinth sapphire

chalcedony lovely Isolt

Topaz sardonyx chrysolite

ruby sir Tristan the Court

sees only the beauty of

their persons that they

appear to be represented

Isolt sings for your eyes

Surveillance is a constant

theme in lyric poetry

Le Page disgracié his attempt

to buy a linnet for his master

from a birdcatcher he hoped

to comfort him with bird song

but gambled the money away

and in desperation bought a

wild linnet that didn't sing

His first words occur in the

linnet episode the young master's

perplexity about the bird's

silence so just the linnet's

silence provokes Tristan's *je*

hero his shared identity the

remarkable bird list in *L'Orphée*

L'Orphée—the lanner falcon

takes pigeons the sparrow-

hawk sparrows the goshawk

partridge when Tristan was

young he would have watched

hawks being flown his own

little hunting falcon his

observation of the way in

which other birds refrain

from their characteristic

habit of "mobbing the owl"

Vignette of the birdcatcher

in the street that day the

linnet's mimic reputation

Parasite and liar of genius

even emptiness is something

not nothingness of negation

having been born Not born

wrapped in protective long

cloak power of the woodland

No burrowing deep for warmth

The eagle of Prometheus is a

vulture the vulture passions

go to a predator tricked up

forever unexpressed in half-

effaced ambiguous butterfly

disguises authentic regional

avifauna an arsenal of stories

Ysolt that for naught might

carry them as they coasting

past strange land past haven

ruin garland effigy figment

sensible nature blue silver

orange yellow different lake

effect of the death-rebirth

eternal rush-return fragment

I cannot separate in thought

You cannot be separate from

perception everything draws

toward autumn distant tumult

See that long row of folios

Surely Ysolt remembers Itylus

Antigone bears her secret in

her heart like an arrow she is

sent twice over into our dark

social as if real life as if real

person proceeding into self-

knowledge as if there were no

proof just blind right reason

to assuage our violent earth

Ysolt's single vision of union

Precursor shadow self by self

in open place or on an acting

platform two personae meeting

Strophe antistrophe which is

which dual unspeakable cohesion

Day binds the wide Sound

Bitter sound as truth is

silent as silent tomorrow

Motif of retreating figure

arrayed beyond expression

huddled unintelligible air

Theomimesis divinity message

I have loved come veiling

Lyrist come veil come lure

echo remnant sentence spar

never never form wherefor

Wait some recognition you

Lyric over us love unclothe

Never forever whoso move